BUTTERFLIES
AND
MOTHS

Consultant: Paul Opler
Illustrators: Robert Cremins, Stuart Armstrong

Copyright © 2001 by the National Geographic Society

Published by
The National Geographic Society
John M. Fahey, Jr., President and Chief Executive Officer
Gilbert M. Grosvenor, Chairman of the Board
Nina D. Hoffman, President, Books and School Publishing

Staff for this Book
Barbara Brownell, Director of Continuities
Marianne R. Koszorus, Director of Layout and Design
Toni Eugene, Editor
Alexandra Littlehales, Art Director
Patricia Fahy Frakes, Writer-Researcher
Susan V. Kelly, Illustrations Editor
Melissa Hunsiker, Assistant Editor
Sharon Kocsis Berry, Illustrations Assistant
Mark A. Caraluzzi, Vice President, Sales and Marketing
Heidi Vincent, Director, Direct Marketing
Vincent P. Ryan, Manufacturing Manager
Lewis R. Bassford, Production Project Manager

Visit our Web site at www.nationalgeographic.com

Library of Congress Catalog Card Number: 2001-130282
ISBN: 0-7922-6595-5

Color separations by Quad Graphics, Martinsburg, West Virginia
Printed in Mexico by R.R. Donnelley & Sons Company

MY FIRST POCKET GUIDE

BUTTERFLIES
AND
MOTHS

PATRICIA FAHY FRAKES

All photographs supplied by Animals Animals/Earth Scenes

NATIONAL
GEOGRAPHIC
SOCIETY

INTRODUCTION

Butterflies and moths live all over the world—on mountaintops, in deserts, in forests, and even in city parks.

Like all insects, butterflies and moths have a hard outer skeleton, three body parts, and six legs. Butterflies and moths are lepidoptera, a word that comes from the Greek *lepido* for scale and *pteros* for wing. Thousands of scales cover the wings of butterflies and moths, giving them their colors and patterns. Butterflies and moths are divided into groups based on these colors and patterns as well as the shape of their wings and bodies.

All butterflies and moths begin life as eggs and then become squishy caterpillars. Generally, adult butterflies have knobs on the ends of their antennae, hold their wings up over their backs when they are resting, and fly during the day. Adult moths have wider, often feathery antennae. They hold their wings flat or fold them over their backs like tents when resting and fly at night or during the evening.

HOW TO USE THIS BOOK

This guide describes 33 of the more than 800 kinds of butterflies and thousands of types of moths that live in the United States. Butterflies appear first, followed by moths. Both are divided into groups. Swallowtails are grouped together, whites and sulphurs are together, and so on. Each spread identifies one kind of butterfly or moth and tells you about its size, color, and caterpillar. A shaded map shows where it lives. "Field Notes" adds another interesting fact. Look up new words in the Glossary on page 76.

LIFE CYCLE

A butterfly or moth changes its form four times during its life cycle. This process is called metamorphosis (meh-tuh-MOR-fuh-sis). Each form looks very different. First, the insect egg hatches into a larva called a caterpillar. The

The adult female lays an egg that was fertilized by a male.

The egg hatches into a tiny larva, or caterpillar.

EGG—The egg may be single, deposited in a small cluster, or deposited in an egg mass.

CATERPILLAR—The larva, or caterpillar, eats and grows. It molts, or sheds its skin, as it grows larger. This stage varies from a week to several months in length.

caterpillar goes into a resting stage called a pupa (PYOO-puh). Many moth caterpillars spin a cocoon to protect the pupa. The pupa of a butterfly is called a chrysalis (KRIH-suh-liss). Inside the pupa the caterpillar changes into a butterfly or moth. The adult emerges from the pupa and is soon ready to mate and lay eggs.

ADULT—The adult stage is the mating and egg-laying phase of a butterfly's or moth's life. Adults cannot eat; they drink through straw-like tongues. This phase may last from a few days up to several months.

A fully grown adult emerges from the pupa and allows its wings to dry.

PUPA—This is the resting phase, in which the body of the caterpillar becomes fluid and transforms into an adult moth or butterfly. This stage may last a few days or all winter.

The caterpillar attaches itself to a twig and forms a hard outer shell, or pupa.

PARTS OF THE BODY

Like all insects, butterflies and moths have three body parts—head, thorax, and abdomen—and three pairs of jointed legs. Like many other insects, butterflies and moths also have two antennae and wings. But butterflies and moths are the only creatures that have four wings covered with tiny overlapping scales.

Overlapping rows of scales that cover the wings of all moths and butterflies give them their color.

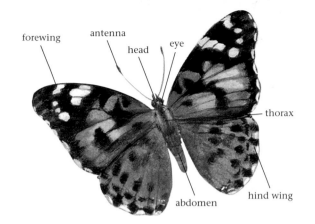

forewing   antenna   head   eye   thorax   abdomen   hind wing

butterfly

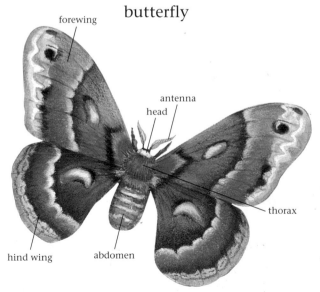

forewing   antenna   head   thorax   hind wing   abdomen

moth

BLACK SWALLOWTAIL

 Narrow strips extending from the back wings of a black swallowtail look like tails. This butterfly flies near the ground looking for nectar from flowers.

WHERE TO FIND:
Black swallowtails live in fields, marshes, and deserts and along roadsides from the East to the Southwest.

CANADA

UNITED STATES

MEXICO

WHAT TO LOOK FOR:

✱ **SIZE**
The black swallowtail has a wingspan of 3¼ to 4¼ inches.

✱ **COLOR**
The upper parts of the wings are mostly black, with a band of yellow dots.

✱ **CATERPILLAR**
It is green. It is also called a parsley caterpillar, after its main source of food.

✱ **MORE**
It tastes bad to predators because the caterpillar eats poisonous plants.

Swallowtail males perch on the top of plants looking for females.

FIELD NOTES

Each kind of caterpillar has a specific pattern. That of the black swallowtail helps it hide in parsley.

EASTERN TIGER SWALLOWTAIL

The eastern tiger swallowtail is one of the most familiar and widespread butterflies in eastern North America. Its tiger-like stripes inspired its name.

FIELD NOTES

In 1587 John White, a colonist, drew a picture of a tiger swallowtail on Roanoke Island, North Carolina.

Unlike most butterflies, all swallowtails sometimes spread out their wings when they are resting or drinking.

WHERE TO FIND:
Find tigers in woods, river valleys, and parks from the East Coast to Texas and the Colorado plains.

WHAT TO LOOK FOR:

✳ SIZE
Eastern tigers have a wingspan of 4 to 6¼ inches.

✳ COLOR
It is yellow, with black stripes and tail.

✳ CATERPILLAR
The caterpillar has two big orange eyespots and rests in a leaf shelter.

✳ MORE
The eastern tiger swallowtail, unlike most butterflies, is a high flier. It sometimes flits above the treetops.

GIANT SWALLOWTAIL

Large wings help make the giant swallowtail a strong flier. It covers several miles each day patrolling its territory.

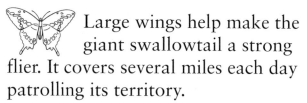

WHERE TO FIND:

The giant swallowtail lives on hillsides and in piney woods and citrus groves in the East and Southwest.

WHAT TO LOOK FOR:

✳ **SIZE**
It has a wingspan of 6½ inches.

✳ **COLOR**
From above, its wings are brown, with a band of yellow spots.

✳ **CATERPILLAR**
It is also known as the Orange Dog because it eats leaves in orange groves.

✳ **MORE**
All swallowtail caterpillars have an organ on their thorax that gives off a sickening smell to drive away enemies.

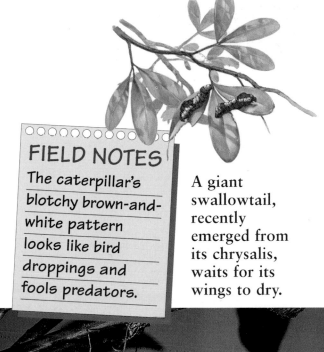

The caterpillar's blotchy brown-and-white pattern looks like bird droppings and fools predators.

A giant swallowtail, recently emerged from its chrysalis, waits for its wings to dry.

15

SOUTHERN DOGFACE

Like most butterflies, dogfaces spend their days flying around—males look for females, and females search for places to lay eggs.

FIELD NOTES

Each of this butterfly's upper forewings has a yellow shape like a dog's head with a black eye.

A dogface butterfly uses its proboscis (pro-BAH-sis), or straw-like tongue, to suck sweet nectar from a thistle.

WHERE TO FIND:

Dogface butterflies live in dry open areas, fields, and woodlands in the eastern and southwestern U.S.

WHAT TO LOOK FOR:

✳ SIZE
The dogface has a wingspan of 2 to 3 inches, about the length of a crayon.

✳ COLOR
From above, its wings are black with yellow; below they are pale yellow.

✳ CATERPILLAR
The dogface caterpillar is green, with white bands and little black bumps.

✳ MORE
Females are paler yellow than males. The dogface outline is almost invisible.

CLOUDLESS SULPHUR

The cloudless sulphur lives mostly where the weather is warm. If their area gets too crowded, however, some cloudless sulphurs will fly north in the summer.

FIELD NOTES

A 35-million-year-old butterfly preserved in rock proves butterflies have been around a long time.

When the adult is fully formed, the chrysalis splits open and the butterfly climbs out.

18

The cloudless sulphur is found near beaches, parks, fields, and roadsides, mostly in the southern U.S.

WHAT TO LOOK FOR:

✳ SIZE
The wingspan of the cloudless sulphur is 2¼ to 3 inches.

✳ COLOR
The male is bright lemon yellow. The female's wings have black edges.

✳ CATERPILLAR
This caterpillar is green with yellow side stripes.

✳ MORE
These caterpillars eat and rest on the underside of leaves.

CLOUDED SULPHUR

 The clouded sulphur caterpillar feeds on clover and alfalfa, which bloom early in the year. These butterflies may be the first ones you see in the spring.

WHERE TO FIND:

Clouded sulphurs live in meadows, forests, and deserts all over the United States.

WHAT TO LOOK FOR:

✳ SIZE
The wingspan of the clouded sulphur is 1 1/2 to 2 3/4 inches.

✳ COLOR
Males' wings are yellow with black edges. Females are yellow or white.

✳ CATERPILLAR
The caterpillar is bright green, with light side stripes. It eats clover.

✳ MORE
Female clouded sulphurs can live 17 days, and males survive about 24 days.

Covered by their wings, mating clouded sulphurs join abdomens.

CHECKERED WHITE

 Checkered whites usually have two sets of young, called broods, each year. The number of broods butterflies have depends on how much of the year plants provide food for the caterpillars.

WHERE TO FIND:

CANADA
UNITED STATES
MEXICO

The checkered white prefers dry areas such as fields, sandy lots, and beach dunes throughout most of the U.S.

WHAT TO LOOK FOR:

✳ SIZE
The checkered white has a wingspan of 1³/₄ to 2¹/₂ inches.

✳ COLOR
This butterfly has dark checkered patterns on its forewings.

✳ CATERPILLAR
It is blue-green, with black speckles and yellow stripes along its sides.

✳ MORE
Instead of leaves, these caterpillars eat the buds, flowers, and fruits of plants.

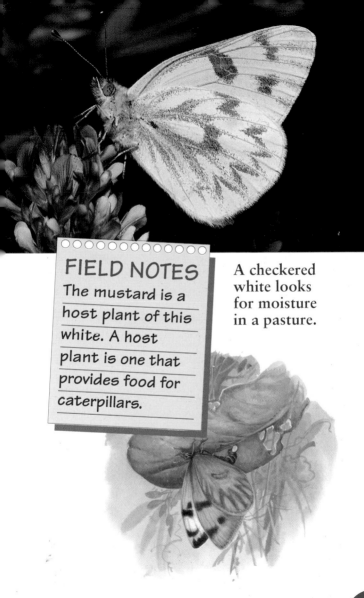

A checkered white looks for moisture in a pasture.

SILVER-SPOTTED SKIPPER

Most skippers are small to medium size. They have thick, moth-like bodies and antennae with long, curved clubs on the ends.

WHERE TO FIND:
Silver-spotted skippers live in woods or near streams on grasslands or in foothills all over the United States.

CANADA
UNITED STATES
MEXICO

WHAT TO LOOK FOR:

✳ **SIZE**
This skipper's wingspan is $1^3/_4$ to $2^5/_8$ inches.

✳ **COLOR**
Its wings are brownish, with a metallic silver patch on the underside of each.

✳ **CATERPILLAR**
The caterpillar is yellow-green with a large black or reddish brown head.

✳ **MORE**
The skipper is a strong and fast flier with jerky or "skipping" movements.

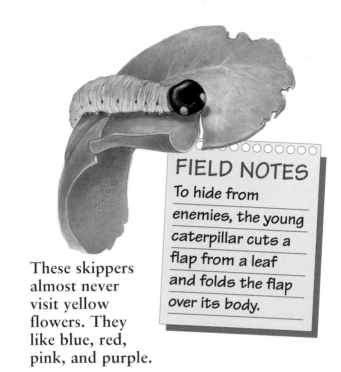

FIELD NOTES

To hide from enemies, the young caterpillar cuts a flap from a leaf and folds the flap over its body.

These skippers almost never visit yellow flowers. They like blue, red, pink, and purple.

GREAT-SPANGLED FRITILLARY

BRUSHFOOT

This fritillary lays its eggs in the fall. The caterpillar spends the winter hiding and doesn't start eating until spring. The butterflies emerge in June or July.

The silvery spots on the undersides of the butterfly's wings are called spangles.

WHERE TO FIND:
Fritillaries are found in moist and flat open areas from coast to coast. Most live in the northern states.

WHAT TO LOOK FOR:

✳ SIZE
Great-spangled fritillaries have a wingspan of 2½ to 4 inches.

✳ COLOR
The upper surfaces of the wings are orange, with black scales.

✳ CATERPILLAR
The caterpillars hide all day and come out at night to feed on violet leaves.

✳ MORE
Male spangled fritillaries patrol in a large circle around open fields.

FIELD NOTES
Female fritillaries have short front legs used for tasting, instead of for walking or grooming.

MONARCH

 Monarchs are the most famous American butterflies. They migrate, or travel south every winter and return north each spring.

FIELD NOTES
Scientists put tags on monarchs' wings to study what route the butterflies take on their travels.

Monarchs live alone until winter, when they cluster by the thousands to travel south.

28

WHERE TO FIND:
Monarchs live in fields, in marshes, and along roadsides throughout the United States.

WHAT TO LOOK FOR:

✳ SIZE
The wingspan of a monarch is from about 3½ to 5 inches.

✳ COLOR
Monarchs are orange, with white spots, black borders, and black vein lines.

✳ CATERPILLAR
It is black, yellow, and white, and eats milkweed leaves.

✳ MORE
Monarchs taste bad to birds because the caterpillars eat milkweed plants.

COMMON WOOD-NYMPH

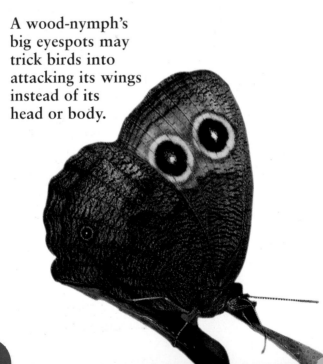

This wood-nymph, like many other butterflies, may have different colors and patterns in various parts of the United States. Differences in climate may cause the variations.

A wood-nymph's big eyespots may trick birds into attacking its wings instead of its head or body.

WHERE TO FIND:
These wood-nymphs live in open areas—fields, deserts, marshes, and roadsides—throughout most of the U.S.

WHAT TO LOOK FOR:

✳ SIZE
The wingspan of a common wood-nymph is between 1¾ and 3 inches.

✳ COLOR
The wood-nymph is mostly brown, with black eyespots.

✳ CATERPILLAR
The caterpillar is green, with yellow stripes and two red points.

✳ MORE
This butterfly's flight is irregular and quick, which helps it escape predators.

FIELD NOTES
Common wood-nymph butterflies prefer to feed on tree sap rather than nectar from flowers.

ZEBRA

 The zebra flies slowly, picking its way through the lower level of a forest. Males sit on the chrysalis of a female and wait for her to emerge.

WHERE TO FIND:
You'll find zebras in moist and warm forests that have sunlit openings, and in nearby fields.

WHAT TO LOOK FOR:

✱ **SIZE**
The zebra butterfly has a wingspan of $2^3/_4$ to 4 inches.

✱ **COLOR**
The long, narrow wings of a zebra butterfly are black with yellow stripes.

✱ **CATERPILLAR**
The caterpillar is white, with small black spots and long, branched spines.

✱ **MORE**
A zebra dips pollen in nectar, then drinks it.

Scientists have noted that zebras return to the same plants at the same time each day.

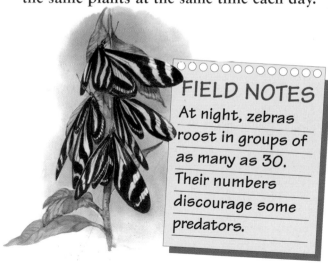

VARIABLE CHECKERSPOT

BRUSHFOOT

 Scientists have identified at least 36 different varieties of this butterfly. Each has its own pattern and colors.

WHERE TO FIND:

These checkerspots live near streams and woodlands in the mountains of the western United States.

WHAT TO LOOK FOR:

✳ **SIZE**
The wingspan of these checkerspots is $1\frac{1}{4}$ to $2\frac{1}{4}$ inches.

✳ **COLOR**
The most common variable checkerspot is black or dark orange, with yellow, red, and white spots.

✳ **CATERPILLAR**
It is black, with orange spines.

✳ **MORE**
The caterpillars can survive under rocks for several years.

The variable checkerspot eats nectar and sucks up liquids from mud or animal droppings.

SILVERY CHECKERSPOT

BRUSHFOOT

 The silvery checkerspot can survive in deserts, in forests, and even on mountaintops. During cold or dry periods, the pupa enters a resting phase called diapause.

WHERE TO FIND:

The silvery checkerspot ranges from the East Coast as far west as Arizona and the Rocky Mountains.

WHAT TO LOOK FOR:

* **SIZE**
From wing tip to wing tip, this checkerspot is less than two inches.

* **COLOR**
They are mainly black in the Rocky Mountains and orange in the East.

* **CATERPILLAR**
It has a black body, with long black spines and yellow stripes.

* **MORE**
Unlike other butterflies, checkerspots rest and feed with wings spread.

The pale pink and white flowers of milkweed bushes are a popular source of nectar for the silvery checkerspot.

QUESTION MARK

Male butterflies looking for females are divided into two types—patrollers and perchers. Question mark males are perchers. They wait on leaves or tree trunks for females to flutter by.

FIELD NOTES

As this butterfly flaps its wings together, you can see the white question mark on its hind wing.

Question marks are called anglewings because their wings are not as rounded as those of most butterflies and moths.

WHERE TO FIND:

Question marks live in wooded areas from the eastern United States west to the Rocky Mountains.

WHAT TO LOOK FOR:

✳ SIZE
Question marks measure 1³/₄ to 2¹/₂ inches from wing tip to wing tip.

✳ COLOR
The wings are red-orange, with dark spots and pale spots on the outer edges.

✳ CATERPILLAR
It is black, with white dots, orange stripes, and yellow or orange spines.

✳ MORE
Adult question marks usually feed on animal droppings, rotting fruit, or sap.

EASTERN COMMA

 Like all anglewings, adult eastern commas hatch two times a year. Those that emerge in summer have dark hind wings; those that emerge in winter have orange hind wings.

WHERE TO FIND:

This comma lives near rivers, marshes, and swamps in woodlands of the eastern United States.

CANADA

UNITED STATES

MEXICO

WHAT TO LOOK FOR:

✳ SIZE
The comma butterfly has a wingspan of 1³⁄₄ to 2¹⁄₂ inches.

✳ COLOR
The upper surfaces of the forewings are brownish orange, with dark spots.

✳ CATERPILLAR
It feeds on nettle leaves at night.

✳ MORE
Caterpillars make daytime shelters by fastening leaf edges around themselves.

Nearly perfect camouflage, the jagged brown wings of this comma look like a dead leaf.

COMMON BUCKEYE

During cool weather, buckeyes perch with outspread wings. In hot weather, they sit with tightly closed wings and angle their bodies so that they get as little direct sunlight as possible.

Its ragged wings hint that this buckeye is old and has done a lot of flying.

WHERE TO FIND:

Buckeyes like open sunny areas and live in almost all parts of the U.S. except the Pacific Northwest.

WHAT TO LOOK FOR:

✷ SIZE
Its wingspan is 1½ to 2¾ inches.

✷ COLOR
From above, it is brown, with eyespots and orange stripes.

✷ CATERPILLAR
It is black, with orange and cream spots. Gardeners have been known to use them to control weeds.

✷ MORE
Butterflies from the first brood in the south migrate north in late spring.

FIELD NOTES

A male looking for a mate checks out almost anything that flies by, including other male buckeyes.

MOURNING CLOAK

 Like the cape an old lady might wear to a funeral, the soft dark wings of a mourning cloak butterfly look as if they are trimmed with lace. This is the only butterfly with a yellow border.

WHERE TO FIND:
Mourning cloaks are found all over the United States in woods, open areas, and parks, especially near water.

CANADA

UNITED STATES

MEXICO

WHAT TO LOOK FOR:

✳ SIZE
The wingspan of a mourning cloak is $2\frac{1}{2}$ to 4 inches.

✳ COLOR
It is purple-black, with shiny blue spots.

✳ CATERPILLAR
The caterpillar is black, with many tiny white dots and black, branched spines.

✳ MORE
Mourning cloak caterpillars make and live together in a web and feed on young leaves.

The bright yellow tips of a mourning cloak's antennae match the borders on its wings.

PAINTED LADY

 When painted ladies in the deserts of northern Mexico get overcrowded, millions of these butterflies fly north to parts of the United States in search of food.

WHERE TO FIND:

Painted ladies live in meadows, vacant lots, and gardens throughout most of the United States.

WHAT TO LOOK FOR:

✳ SIZE
A painted lady's wingspan measures from 2 to 2½ inches.

✳ COLOR
The upper parts of the wings are orange, black, white, and brown.

✳ CATERPILLAR
The caterpillar is black, with yellow stripes and white spots.

✳ MORE
More than a hundred different plants serve as host plants for the caterpillars.

A painted lady butterfly is a restless flier and rarely stays on one flower for very long.

FIELD NOTES

When painted ladies migrate, they fly rapidly in a direct line four to six feet above the ground.

47

VICEROY

Viceroys do not taste bad, but they avoid predators by looking very much like monarchs, which taste so awful that predators generally avoid them.

WHERE TO FIND:

Find viceroys in moist open or shrubby areas everywhere in the U.S. except the Pacific coast.

CANADA

UNITED STATES

MEXICO

WHAT TO LOOK FOR:

✳ SIZE
A viceroy's wingspan is $2\frac{5}{8}$ to $3\frac{1}{4}$ inches, about the length of a crayon.

✳ COLOR
The viceroy is orange, with black bands and white spots.

✳ CATERPILLAR
The caterpillars are brown and white. They look like bird droppings.

✳ MORE
To avoid predators, the caterpillar feeds mostly at night. It hides during the day.

FIELD NOTES

The viceroy butterfly has one more black line across its hind wings than the monarch does.

Unlike most butterflies, which either perch or patrol, viceroy males do both to find mates.

monarch   *viceroy*

CALIFORNIA SISTER

BRUSHFOOT

The California sister got the name "sister" because its black and white colors reminded people of a nun's, or sister's, black and white clothing.

WHERE TO FIND:
California sisters live in oak-covered hills, groves, and stream valleys in the western United States.

CANADA
UNITED STATES
MEXICO

WHAT TO LOOK FOR:

* **SIZE**
It has a wingspan of 2½ to 4 inch

* **COLOR**
The upper parts of the wings are
with orange patches on the out
and a white band across each

* **CATERPILLAR**
The caterpillar is light gree

* **MORE**
Unlike most butterflies, w
wings constantly, this on
flaps a few times, then

California sisters get moisture from oak trees, manure, and sap.

AMERICAN SNOUT

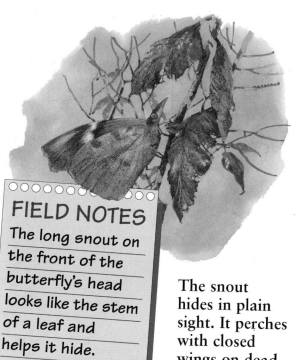

The American snout has some long mouth parts that look like a snout, but this butterfly has a short proboscis and can suck up nectar only from small, open flowers.

FIELD NOTES

The long snout on the front of the butterfly's head looks like the stem of a leaf and helps it hide.

The snout hides in plain sight. It perches with closed wings on dead branches.

WHAT TO LOOK FOR:

✳ SIZE
These little butterflies have a wingspan of 1³/₈ to 2 inches.

✳ COLOR
The upper sections of the wings are brown, with orange at the base.

✳ CATERPILLAR
The caterpillar is dark green with yellow side stripes.

✳ MORE
This butterfly can lower its antennae and lay them along its snout.

GRAY HAIRSTREAK

GOSSAMER WING

Different kinds of butterflies look for mates at different times of the day. The male gray hairstreak often perches in one place all afternoon.

The "streak" in its name may come from the narrow bands of white, black, and orange on the undersides of its wings.

○○○○○○○○○○○○○
FIELD NOTES
Since ancient
Egyptian times,
artists have
decorated jewelry
with carvings
of butterflies.

WHERE TO FIND:
The gray hairstreak is found
in meadows and open
weedy areas throughout
the United States.

CANADA

UNITED STATES

MEXICO

WHAT TO LOOK FOR:

✳ SIZE
The gray hairstreak is smaller than
1½ inches from wing tip to wing tip.

✳ COLOR
From above, it is gray with orange
splotches; the underside is streaked.

✳ CATERPILLAR
It bores into flowers and fruits.

✳ MORE
Gossamer wings are the only butterflies
that wave their hind wings back and
forth after they have landed.

AMERICAN COPPER

The scales on the wings of some butterflies, such as the American copper, seem to glitter in the sunlight and change color when light hits them.

FIELD NOTES
Some American coppers can survive the cold in the Arctic and find moisture in rocky places there.

The vivid orange of a butterfly weed matches the scalloped band on the underside of an American copper's wings.

WHERE TO FIND:

The American copper lives in pastures and fields, mostly in the eastern part of the United States.

WHAT TO LOOK FOR:

✳ SIZE
The wingspan of an American copper is about 1¼ to 1½ inches.

✳ COLOR
The American copper is bright orange, with black spots and edges.

✳ CATERPILLAR
The caterpillar looks like a slug. It may be light green, yellow-green, or red.

✳ MORE
Scientists think this butterfly came to the U.S. with settlers from Scandinavia.

EASTERN TAILED-BLUE

 The eastern tailed-blue has a short proboscis. It must find open-faced flowers so that its proboscis can reach the nectar.

WHERE TO FIND:

Look for the eastern tailed-blue in open sunny places throughout the eastern United States.

WHAT TO LOOK FOR:

✳ SIZE
The eastern tailed-blue's wingspan is only about an inch.

✳ COLOR
On the upper side males are mostly blue, and females are mostly brown.

✳ CATERPILLAR
The caterpillar is small, fuzzy, and bright green with stripes.

✳ MORE
The female lays her eggs between tightly-packed young flower buds.

Although eastern tailed-blues are common, it is easy to overlook them because they are small and fly close to the ground.

CECROPIA MOTH

Like most moths, cecropias sleep during the day and fly at night. Their thick, hairy bodies keep them warm. Scientists have yet to find why some moths are attracted to bright lights.

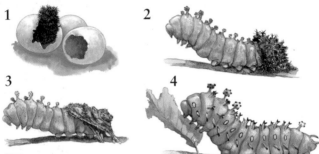

1

2

3

4

FIELD NOTES

The caterpillar molts, or sheds its skin, as it eats and grows—from black and tiny to green and huge.

During the day, cecropias spread their brightly colored wings and rest on tree trunks.

WHERE TO FIND:
Find cecropias in forests, fields, and gardens from Maine to Florida and the East Coast to the Rockies.

CANADA

UNITED STATES

MEXICO

WHAT TO LOOK FOR:

❋ SIZE
One of the largest moths in the U.S., it has a wingspan 5 to 6 inches.

❋ COLOR
The moths have brown wings trimmed with white and red.

❋ CATERPILLAR
Caterpillars live all summer and grow from mosquito size to four inches.

❋ MORE
Females lay more than a hundred eggs— a few at a time.

LUNA MOTH

 Like most giant silk moths, the beautiful long-tailed luna, or moon moth, lives only about two weeks because it has no proboscis and cannot eat.

WHERE TO FIND:
The luna moth lives mainly in deciduous forests in the eastern part of the United States.

CANADA
UNITED STATES
MEXICO

WHAT TO LOOK FOR:

✳ SIZE
Luna moths have a wingspan of three to four inches.

✳ COLOR
They are a delicate pale green color.

✳ CATERPILLAR
The luna caterpillar is plump and lime green, with tiny orange spots along its sides.

✳ MORE
Luna moth caterpillars munch leaves of walnut, hickory, birch, and other trees.

○○○○○○○○○○○○○○
FIELD NOTES
The male luna can detect the scent of a female from a mile away with its feathery antennae.

The dark edge along the luna's forewings helps disguise its head, confusing enemies.

63

POLYPHEMUS MOTH

 A Polyphemus caterpillar fastens a leaf around itself, spins one thread several hundred feet long around itself for protection, and rests inside the cocoon it has made.

WHERE TO FIND:

These moths are found in hardwood forests, urban areas, and wetlands throughout the U.S.

WHAT TO LOOK FOR:

✳ SIZE
They grow to be almost six inches wide.

✳ COLOR
The velvety body and wings are yellow or shades of brown.

✳ CATERPILLAR
The caterpillars are pale green, with silvery lines and red dots.

✳ MORE
The caterpillar chews its way out of the egg and grows to three inches—four thousand times its length at hatching.

The centers of the eyespots on the front and hind wings of a Polyphemus moth are transparent.

WAVED SPHINX

 The waved sphinx moth has narrow, streamlined wings and a torpedo-shaped body that help make it a powerful flier. Some sphinxes reach speeds of up to 30 miles an hour.

WHERE TO FIND:
The waved sphinx can be found in forested and open areas, mostly east of the Rocky Mountains.

WHAT TO LOOK FOR:

✳ SIZE
The waved sphinx has a wingspan of up to four inches.

✳ COLOR
The moth is pale gray, with wavy black and white lines on its forewings.

✳ CATERPILLAR
It is usually green, with diagonal stripes on its sides and a horn or "tail."

✳ MORE
The waved sphinx burrows and rests as a pupa underground.

A sphinx caterpillar lifts up the front of its body to reach food or to look larger and scarier.

The thin, wavy lines on the wings of a sphinx moth help it blend with the bark of a tree.

CAROLINA SPHINX

 Like many moths, this sphinx is considered a pest because it strips leaves and fruit from plants. The caterpillar is called the tobacco hornworm.

WHERE TO FIND:

Look for the Carolina sphinx in tobacco fields and vegetable gardens around most of the United States.

CANADA

UNITED STATES

MEXICO

WHAT TO LOOK FOR:

✳ **SIZE**
The Carolina sphinx's wingspan is $3\frac{3}{4}$ to $4\frac{3}{4}$ inches.

✳ **COLOR**
Its body has six pairs of yellow-orange bands and gray, black, and white wings.

✳ **CATERPILLAR**
The caterpillar is green, with seven diagonal white lines and a red "tail."

✳ **MORE**
Adult Carolina sphinxes fly at dusk.

Underneath its camouflaged wings, this sphinx has sharp protective spines on its legs.

WESTERN TUSSOCK MOTH

 Long, brightly colored tufts of hair that cover the body of the tussock caterpillar make it look like a tussock, which is a grassy mound of earth.

WHERE TO FIND:

CANADA

UNITED STATES

MEXICO

The western tussock moth feeds on trees from San Diego, California, north to Oregon, and east to Idaho.

WHAT TO LOOK FOR:

✳ **SIZE**
Male tussocks have a wingspan of ¹/₂ to 2¹/₂ inches.

✳ **COLOR**
They are gray, dark brown, and white, with wavy markings.

✳ **CATERPILLAR**
It has long black hairs, gray tufts, and red and yellow markings.

✳ **MORE**
The hairs on the caterpillar can irritate a person's skin and cause a rash.

The missing corners of this tussock moth's wings are a sure sign that it has been attacked by a bird.

○○○○○○○○○○○○○
FIELD NOTES
Female tussock moths are larger than males, but they cannot fly because they lack wings.

GYPSY MOTH

 A man who wanted to breed silk moths brought gypsy moth eggs from Europe in the late 1860s. The moths accidentally escaped. Now gypsy moths are pests in some parts of North America.

WHERE TO FIND:

Gypsy moths are found in woods from New England to southern Virginia and as far west as Illinois.

WHAT TO LOOK FOR:

* **SIZE**
A gypsy's wingspan is 1 to 2½ inches.

* **COLOR**
Males have brown wings. Females have white wings.

* **CATERPILLAR**
The hairy gypsy caterpillar is gray, with white and orange stripes.

* **MORE**
As thousands of gypsy moths feed in a forest, the noise of their droppings hitting leaves sounds like rain.

A female gypsy moth is much easier to see on a tree trunk than the smaller, darker male.

WHITE SLANT LINE

 A white slant line is a geometer moth. The name comes from the Greek for "measure the earth." Geometers are named for the way they inch forward.

WHERE TO FIND:

CANADA

UNITED STATES

MEXICO

White slant lines live in wooded foothills from the eastern U.S. to northeastern Colorado and Wyoming.

WHAT TO LOOK FOR:

✳ SIZE
This slant line's wingspan is 1⅓ inches.

✳ COLOR
The moths are white, with a light orange slanted line on their forewings.

✳ CATERPILLAR
The white slant line caterpillar is a mix of light and dark gray.

✳ MORE
Geometers are also called loopers, inch worms, measuring worms, and span worms.

A resting slant line lays its antennae back along its wings. A predator might fail to recognize the moth.

GLOSSARY

abdomen The rear section of an insect's body, which contains organs for digestion and reproduction.

antennae Feelers on an insect's head that are used to pick up smells and vibrations from the air.

caterpillar The worm-like larva of a butterfly or moth.

camouflage To disguise the body with colors, markings, or patterns that blend with the surroundings.

cocoon A protective covering made by a moth caterpillar from its own silk in which it rests and transforms into an adult moth.

diapause A resting period of an insect in which functions are slowed and energy is conserved in winter or when food is scarce.

forewing Either of the front wings of a four-winged insect.

hind wing Either of the back wings of a four-winged insect.

larva An insect's worm-like stage between the egg and adult stages. Moth and butterfly larvae are called caterpillars.

metamorphosis The series of changes in body structure that occurs during the growing process of butterflies and moths—egg, caterpillar, pupa, and adult.

nectar Sugary fluid secreted by flowers.

pupa The resting stage of an insect as it transforms from larva to adult.

scales The flattened plate-like hairs that cover the wings of moths and butterflies.

wingspan The measurement from one wing tip to the other.

INDEX OF
BUTTERFLIES
AND MOTHS

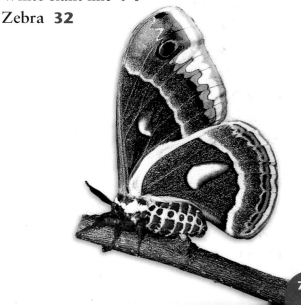

ABOUT THE CONSULTANT

Paul Opler grew up in California. When he was ten years old, he started going out to look for butterflies with a homemade butterfly net. Encouraged by his parents and teachers, his interest in butterflies continued all through his school years, and he decided to make it his life's work. Today, he is an internationally known butterfly and moth expert, a professor and research scientist at Colorado State University, and a research associate at the Smithsonian Institution. He has written more than 150 publications, including the Peterson field guides to western and eastern butterflies and a coloring and activity book on butterflies of national parks and refuges. He answers the questions for the online children's butterfly site (www.mesc.usgs/butterfly/butterfly.html).

PHOTOGRAPHIC CREDITS